HOLLAND

500 Colour Photos

BONECHI

Distribution:

NILSSON & LAMM B.V.
Pampuslaan 212 - 214
Postbus 195
1380 AD WEESP (HOLLAND)
E-mail: Geotoer@nilsson-lamm.nl

Telefoon 0294 494949
Telefax 0294 494455

Publication created and designed by Casa Editrice Bonechi
Project manager Monica Bonechi
Photographic research by Marco Bonechi
Graphic design by Marco Bonechi *and* Serena de Leonardis
Video layout and editing by Giorgio Montinari
Text by Giovanna Magi *and* Giorgio Montinari
Drawings and Maps: Stefano Benini

© Copyright by Casa Editrice Bonechi, via Cairoli 18/b Firenze - Italia
Tel +39 055576841 - Fax +39 0555000766
E-mail:bonechi@bonechi.it - Internet:www.bonechi.it

Printed in Italy by Centro Stampa Editoriale Bonechi.

Photographs from the Archives of Casa Editrice Bonechi *taken by*
Marco Bonechi, Ronald Glaudemans, Joop ten Veen, Paolo Giambone, Andrea Pistolesi, Marco Banti.
*The photographs on pages 70 bottom left, 71 top right, 72 bottom (H. van den Leeden), 48 top (Schliack),
85 top (G. Vetten), 142 top (Van Dam), 57 bottom, 109 top right (D. Lemke), 6 bottom,
were kindly provided by* Nederlands Bureau voor Toerisme.
The photographs on pages 24, 25, 26, 27, 28 were kindly provided by
Rijksmuseum Stichting, Amsterdam.
The photographs on pages 62, 63, 64, 70 top, 71 bottom are by Andrea Innocenti.
The photograph on pages 91 centre, is by A. M. van der Heyden.

ISBN 88-476-0214-9

* * *

A BRIEF HISTORICAL OUTLINE

When the Romans reached the mouth of the Rhine River in the year 50 B.C., they found themselves in a flat, sandy region, chilled by the cold north winds and prone to frequent flooding by the North Sea. They also found several tribes, perhaps of Germanic origin, who lived by hunting and fishing. The central region was occupied by the Batavians, as mentioned by Plinius, while the Franks, a Celtic race, had settled in the south, and the Frisians thrived in the north. The Saxons, the most Germanic of all, lived mainly in the region northeast of the Rhine. Nevertheless, despite their common origin, these populations differed greatly from one another. At first, it seemed that the Roman conquest was a boon to all, but soon revolts broke out; the first to rebel were the Frisians, followed by the Batavians. Both tribes joined together in 68-70 A.D. under the leadership of Claudius Julius Civilis, who was the organizer of the whole revolt. Nevertheless, the Romans were able to keep their legions in the territory for over three centuries – it was not until 300 A.D. that the pressure of the Germanic tribes began to make headway against the Roman domination. The Batavians were wiped out almost immediately and only the Frisians in the north managed to survive and oppose the Frankish onslaught. It was just as hard to Christianize the region as it had been to conquer it. In the south the conversion of the heathen was carried on by the Merovingian kings, in the north by two Anglo-Saxon missionaries, St. Willibrord and St. Boniface.

Yet, the Frisians, for example, stubbornly clung to their paganism for at least two hundred years. During the Carolingian domination the emphasis on evangelization continued. On one hand, Charlemagne used force to subdue the Frisians and Saxons, while on the other, he gave them the laws that would govern them for centuries. At the same time, he divided the country into various provinces ruled by counts, who were actually vassals of the emperor. But even at this time the Dutch not only had to wage war against the elements, the most terrible of which was the sea, but they also had to stand up to just as dreadful human foes, the Vikings, whose savage incursions and forays meant the sacking, looting, and devastation of the Dutch towns. In 841 Charlemagne died and his vast Carolingian empire began to fall apart. Several power struggles later, Holland, and with her, Belgium found themselves part of the Germanic empire. During the Middle Ages, the Netherlands existed as a group of regions under the rule of the Counts of Gelder and Holland, the Duke of Brabant, and the Bishop of Utrecht. This period of Dutch history is mainly characterized by the internecine fighting among the various townships, by now wealthy and powerful in their own right, although foreign dynasties, such as those of Wittelsbach, Bohemia, Luxembourg, and Burgundy, would later overcome the local ones. The Burgundy dynasty managed to dominate all the others when Philip the Bold married Margaret of Flanders; his grandson, Philip the

Panoramic vista of the fields which extend as far as the eye can see between Hoorn and Edam.

Good, went about consolidating his grandfather's power by creating a huge state which took in all the other provinces and setting up a powerful regular army. He established provincial courts (administrative and law), and was also responsible for the creation of the office of stathouder a kind of governor who officially represented the emperor, wielding both political and military authority. Philip the Good was succeeded by Charles the Bold who died in a battle against the Swiss in the year 1477. Charles was succeeded by his daughter, Marie of Burgundy, who having married Maximilian of Austria, son of the emperor Frederick III, brought the Netherlands under Austrian domination. In 1500, Charles, the son of Isabella of Castile and Ferdinand of Aragon, was born in Gand. He was king of Spain by way of his mother, and Duke of Burgundy and the Netherlands by way of his father. In 1519 upon the death of his grandfather, Maximilian of Austria, he was elected Holy Roman Emperor and at this point he could truly boast that the sun never set on his empire. As comprehensive and tolerant as he was in political matters, Charles V, a devout and zealous Catholic, could not accept the Protestant religion of the Netherlands. It was under his reign – as enlightened as it was in other respects – that the religious persecutions got underway. At the same time, the development of the Reformation and the resulting Dutch opposition to the Catholic religion, had a dual effect, for it was at the same time a fight to uphold a principle and a way of opposing the foreign invaders. In 1555, following Charles V's abdication, Charles' son, Philip, rose to the throne. He was completely unlike his father. Having grown up in Spain, he spoke neither French nor Dutch, and worse still, he had no inkling of what the problems of his subjects were. In short, his way of thinking, cultural background, and character were all thoroughly Spanish. A tremendous unbridgeable gap developed between Philip and the Dutch people who in the meantime had become more and more firmly entrenched in the Calvinist doctrines. This led to the formation of a movement to oppose the heavy-handed Spanish interference into Dutch affairs. The leaders of the anti-Spanish movement were the Count of Egmont, the Count of Hornes, and the Prince of Orange, William of Nassau, called "Willem de Zwijger," that is to say, William the Silent, because he used to keep his mouth shut and his ears wide open. During the months of August-September 1566 the exasperation and rage of the people boiled over. Churches and monasteries were sacked, profaned, burnt, and destroyed. Philip's reaction was swift and terrible. He sent the Duke of Alba, otherwise known as the "Iron Duke" at the head of a mighty army to crush the country under a reign of terror. The result was numerous executions, among which those of the Count of Egmont and the Count of Hornes, the death sentence was inflicted on William of Orange (who in the meantime had fled the country), and the rebel cities were sacked and burned down. This marked the start of a long and bloody war between Spain and the Netherlands, still torn by the fierce internal conflicts between Catholics, Lutherans, and Calvinists then raging. The outcome of this bitter struggle was the Union of Utrecht of 1579 which established the full autonomy of the Seven Provinces of the North and designated Dutch as the official language of the country. In 1584, in Delft, a Frenchman named Balthazar Gérard assassinated William the Silent and the leadership of the opposition passed to his son Maurice – who repeatedly offered the Dutch crown to Henry III of France and Elizabeth of England, trying to exploit their fierce rivalry with Spain. Things took a turn for the better when the Dutch made up their minds to rely on themselves and on themselves alone; thus the Republic of the United Provinces with the States General at the head of it was born from the

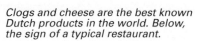

Clogs and cheese are the best known Dutch products in the world. Below, the sign of a typical restaurant.

to Java to load their cargoes of precious spices. Then, in 1602 Johan von Oldenbarnevelt founded the East India Company, soon followed by the West India Company in 1621. From far-off Oriental and African trade routes, Holland's merchant ships brought home spices, salt, gold, rice, ivory, and perfumes. The Dutch who stayed home were kept busy too – they were engaged in weaving, ship building, herring fishing, whale hunting, diamond cutting, and ceramic making. Merchants and the middle class in general came to dominate the whole structure of Dutch society. The economic boom was paralleled by a cultural flowering, especially in the fields of art and philosophic thought. Little Holland gave the world geniuses such as Erasmus, Spinoza, Grotius, Rembrandt, Frans Hals, and Hobbema. The exciting intellectual atmosphere and the stimulating liberty in the intellectual world even attracted a great thinker like Descartes who spent 20 years of his life in Holland and wrote his Discourse on Method in Leyden. Great spiritual discoveries went hand in hand with great geographical discoveries: Tasmania, New Zealand, the Cape of Good Hope, and Cape Horn were discovered and explored. A group of Dutch pilgrims settled in the colony of New Amsterdam, later known as New York. All of this wealth and splendor began to excite the jealousy of England, Holland's biggest rival on the seas. After numerous skirmishes, Cromwell got the English Parliament to approve the Navigation Act in 1651. It provided that foreign ships could only unload goods from their own territories in English ports and in addition were obliged to render homage to Britain's naval power. In short, the English demanded that their supremacy be recognized. The constant battles they were compelled to wage against the British wore down the Dutch people's resistance and self-confidence. A number of their colonies were lost and several ports could no longer be considered safe. After England, it was France's turn to undermine the shaky Dutch empire. Louis XIV, in keeping with his expansionist aims, managed to mobilize several anti-Dutch powers, thereby forcing the Netherlands to take part in several exhausting joint wars. It was not until 1697 and the Peace Treaty of Ryswick that the long struggle finally drew to an end. At that point, the current Stathouder of Holland,

ashes of the Union of Utrecht. Under the command of Prince Maurice the united army aided by the British fleet was able to defeat the Spaniards on both sea and land, so that in 1609 Philip was forced to acknowledge the independence of the Dutch republic and sign a twelve year truce with its representatives. Under the Treaty of Westphalia signed in 1648, all of the European powers recognized the new state, although this did much to increase the hostility of the great naval powers, mainly England. Thus Holland, her independent status no longer threatened, could concentrate her efforts on economic development, the result of which was that shortly afterwards, she became the richest state in Europe. Dutch ships sailed the high seas in direct competition with the British fleet and when Spain refused access to the Portuguese ports, the Dutch went off

The bicycle is the Dutch people's favorite form of transport.

A typical view of the Dutch countryside. Some skaters on a frozen lake in the winter.

William III of Orange, as husband of Mary, daughter of James II, was already king of England and could justly rejoice in the diplomatic victory he had been able to procure, i.e. the Netherlands, England, Prussia, and Austria were allied together in a joint effort against the Catholic countries, France and Spain. When William died in 1702, the Orange dynasty died with him and the leadership passed to the Orange-Nassau fine (which still rules Holland). Throughout the 18th century there was an alternation of republican and monarchist sentiment, whereby creating fertile terrain for the new ideas filtering in from revolutionary France. The army of the Convention entered the Netherlands, thus putting an end to the existence of the almost 200 year old Republic of the Seven Provinces. The last of the stathouders, William V, crossed the English Channel and sought refuge in England. The state born from this insurrection in 1795 was known as the Batavian Republic, but it was extremely short-lived, for in 1806 Napoleon Bonaparte set his brother Louis upon the Dutch throne. Louis was able to win the affection of his subjects in a brief time, but the "continental blockade" brought about the rapid decline of Dutch overseas trade. The Netherlands was thus annexed to the empire and in 1810 became a province of France. In 1813 the dynasty of the Orange was restored, and on November 30 the son of William V, who had taken the name William I, landed in Scheveningen. After the French defeat at Waterloo, the joint forces decided to reunite the northern and southern Low Countries in a single realm. The decision was sanctioned by the Congress of Vienna in 1815 and Holland, Belgium, and the Duchy of Luxembourg were united in the Reign of the Low Countries under the rule of William I of Orange-Nassau. This proved to be a terrible mistake, since after more than two hundred years of political, linguistic, religious, and economic separation, the northern and southern provinces were divided by an unbridgeable gap: the northern population was Protestant and spoke Dutch, the southerners Catholic and spoke French, while the Flemish spoke Dutch, but they too were Catholic. These factors were further complicated by the political aspira tions of the English who, fearing a strong naval rival on the North Sea, did their best to exploit the rebellious uprisings in Belgium and strongly backed its independence movement. This diplomatic coup reached its goal when in

1831 after a pacific revolution, Belgium broke away from the Low Countries and Leopold of Saxe-Coburg, grandson of the English king George IV, rose to the throne. Under the next two monarchs, William II and William III, Holland enjoyed a long stretch of relative economic well-being and renewed expansion. Agriculture, industry, and commerce once more flourished, Indonesia was colonized, and social reforms could be enacted. The neutrality proclaimed by Holland in World War I did much to further her political prestige. William III's reign was of brief duration and his daughter Wilhelmina soon succeeded him. Then, during the night between May 9 and May 10, 1940, despite the country's declared neutrality, Hitler's troops overran the Dutch borders and started bombing the country. No previous warning and no formal declaration of war had been issued. This shameful event was followed by five long years of blood and tears for the Dutch people who were encouraged to resist bravely by their Queen from her London exile. Finally, in 1945 the country was liberated. In 1948, after a reign which had spanned almost 50 years, Wilhelmina abdicated in favor of her daughter Juliana who, starting from the post-war period and continuing up to our day, has been witness to Holland's rebirth and renewed splendor.

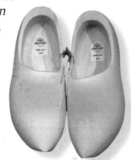

The De Kat mill at Zaanse Schans.

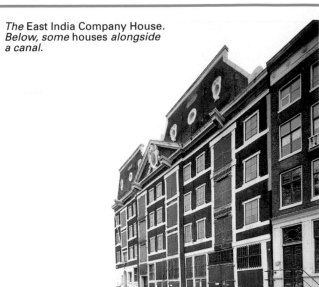

The East India Company House.
Below, some houses *alongside a canal.*

A view of some typical houses in Amsterdam and their reflections on the water.

AMSTERDAM

We have no real information about the foundation of Amsterdam. According to legend, two fishermen, accompanied by their dog, were shipwrecked in a violent storm while on a fishing trip. They set about building a refuge in the swamps where the River Amstel flows into the estuary of the Zuider Zee (also called the Ij) and the settlement founded by the two fishermen and their families who later joined them, is said to be the origin of what we call Amsterdam today. Since the village was located at the mouth of the Amstel River, it was also necessary to construct a dam to protect their homes from the stormy waters. This was the derivation of the city's name, Amstelledamme (dam on the Amstel), which was later changed to Amsterdam. The city is mentioned for the first time by its original name in a charter dated October 27, 1275 in which Floris V granted tax exemption and the right of free trade to its citizens. Amsterdam, which drew its life and livelihood from the water, developed so quickly that by the 17th century it stood out among all the others as queen of the high seas. Diamond cutting and the importation of colonial products such as tea, coffee, tobacco, and cocoa were her major activities. The **East and West India companies** set up their headquarters in Amsterdam, at which time it was embellished with magnificent mansions along the three huge concentric canals encircling the whole town. Then Amsterdam's splendor began to wane just about the same time that England and France were on the rise as sea powers. Subjected to Bonaparte's dominion, Amsterdam was the first Dutch city (1813) to rebel against the foreign yoke. She headed the movement which later founded the independent kingdom of Holland. Overrun and occupied by the Nazis in 1940, along with the other Dutch cities, Amsterdam would regain her freedom only

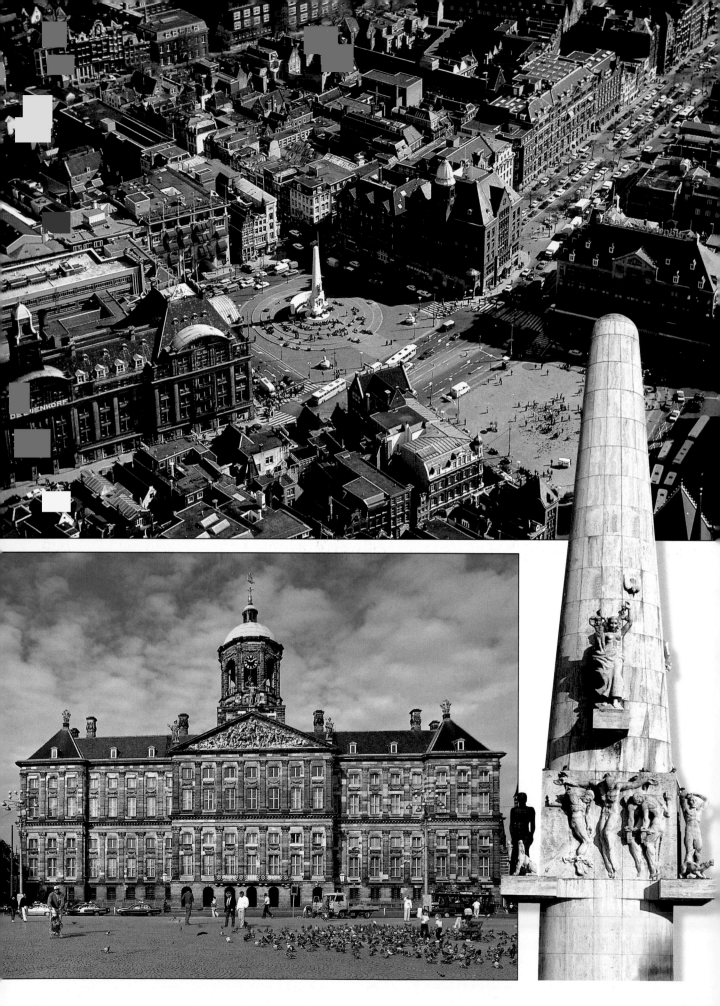

five years later. The **Dam**, a huge, irreg-ularly-shaped square, is the heart of the city. "Dam" means dyke in Dutch and in fact, it was here that hundreds of years ago Dutch fishermen built their homes so that they would be protected from the perilous waters of the river. Thereafter, the city developed outwards from this point. Even though the square is today mostly filled with modern buildings (some of rather questionable taste), there are also two old buildings of great interest, the **Royal Palace**, and the Nieuwe Kerk. The palace, a fine example of the Dutch classic style, was built between 1648 and 1655 upon a foundation of 13.659 pylons. The **Nieuwe Kerk**, of which only the right side is visible, was rebuilt in 1452 after a great fire had destroyed it along with most of the city. The **Monument to the Liberation** rising in the middle, was built in 1956 by J. Radecker. It was built in memory of the Dutch who perished in World War II. The monument con-

tains 12 urns, each of which is filled with soil from eleven Dutch localities and one with soil from Indonesia. There are different versions to account for the origin of the women who dedicate themselves to good works known as Beguines. Some say they were pious women who preferred the cloistered but less rigid life of the Beguinage to the irrevocable vows of the convent. At any rate, once they had entered the institution they dedicated their lives to teach-ing and

On the previous page: a panoramic vista of the Dam, *the* Royal Palace, *the* Liberation monument. *Above, a detail of the* frontispiece *of the Royal Palace; below, the* Citizen's Hall, *a view of the* statue of Atlas *on the back wall of the hall and a detail of the* frieze *in the Tribunal* Hall.

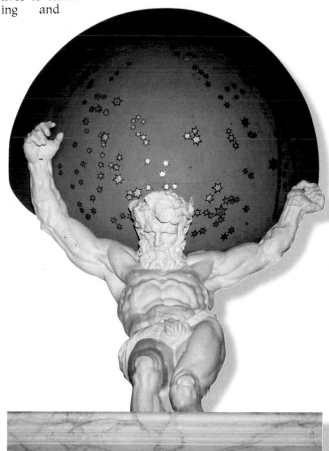

caring for the sick. Others say that the Beguines were originally the widows of fishermen who retired to this life dedicating themselves to charity and needlework. Whatever the origin of the institution, the **Beguinage** of Amsterdam (founded in 1346) is one of the finest in the Netherlands. Its courtyard, an oasis of peace in the heart of the city, dates from the 14th century and is surrounded by houses built in the 15th and 16th centuries. Because of alterations and rebuilding over the centuries, the façades and appearance of the houses are often those of the 17th and 18th centuries, but a number of them are much older: the one at No. 34, for example, dates from the 14th century and still has its medieval wooden front intact. After the religious turmoil which followed the Reformation, many of these houses were used as secret Roman Catholic churches. One of the Beguinage's points of interest is the grave of a Beguine called Cornelia Arens, who asked to be buried in the gutter in order to do penance for the members of her family who had turned Protestant. On May 2 every year there is a picturesque ceremony in which today's Beguines strew her grave with flowers and sand.

Along the **Oudezijds Voorburgwal** are numerous examples of typical Dutch dwellings. The design of the house at No. 19, built in 1656 as the stone high on the façade says, shows the richest sense of imagination. It has two huge

Above, view of the Begijnhof; *below, a view of the* Oudezijds Voorburgwal *and the* House of the Three Canals.

dolphins, the largest in all Amsterdam, on either side of the so-called "neck gable" which crowns the house. The dolphins are linked by huge strings containing countless shells, yet another example of the life and emblems of the sea which recur in various forms throughout the architecture of Amsterdam.

There is another example of a house with a neck gable at No. 187 Oudezijds Voorburgwal. This dwelling, built in 1663 and belonging originally to a merchant, is also called – understandably – the house with the "façade of pillars": the first four pillars are of the Tuscan order, the next four are Ionic and the top two are Corinthian, all being made from brick. At the top are two nude statues of an Indian and a Negro, leaning against a pile of merchandise, including ropes and rolls of tobacco. A scroll in the center hides the arm of the hoist used to lift goods up to the storeroom, the door of which is below: the storeroom and private residence of the merchant were thus one and the same building. The façade was richly adorned with festoons of fruit, scrolls and ovals. The more sober and simple the lower part of the house was, the richer the decoration on the upper section.

The one at No. 14, built in the first years of the 17th centu-

ry, is outstanding. The house has what is known as a "step gable" and many windows with shutters all over the façade, as if the people who lived here wanted to enjoy the sunlight as much as possible, letting it flood into all the rooms. The rooms themselves were sober, the furnishings few, the floor uncovered: a simple place in all respects. The unusual and striking shape of the **Sint Anthoniespoort** (St. Antony's Gate) makes it recognizable from miles away. The gate, originally the eastern entrance to the city, is the only one extant from the Middle Ages. In 1617 it was turned into the Public Weighing Station, or Waag, and closed off by five massive towers. Although the ground floor continued to be used as the weighing station until 1819, the upper floor became the headquarters of some of the local crafts guilds. Since 1975 the Waag has been occupied by the city's interesting Jewish Museum.

The Amstel is the river which crosses a good part of the city and which gave the city its name. It was on the banks of the Amstel, as we have seen, that the first settlers founded what was to be the city of Amsterdam, and the names of the streets in this, the oldest part of the city, recall their origins. Running parallel to the Amstel on either side are two large canals, known collectively as the Voorburgwal, a name referring to the wall or moat in front of the city. The whole canal system linking Amsterdam is spanned by numerous bridges, but the **Magere Brug** (which means either Skinny Bridge or the bridge designed by Mager) is the most picturesque and is the only wooden drawbridge left on the Amstel. Ian Wagenaar,

Above, the Waag or Sint Anthoniespoort.
Below, two views of the Oudezijds Voorburgwal.

Above, a view of a canal; *in the center, the* Muziektheater; *below, the* Magere Brug.

the city's historian, wrote that in his time (around the year 1765) there were no less than 250 bridges in Amsterdam, half of them made of wood. Originally built as a narrow footbridge, the Magere Brug was first enlarged and then had a movable section built into it in the center. Finally in 1772 it was converted into a double drawbridge. Standing on its slender arches, the bridge has an elegant appearance, but at night, when it is all lit up, it takes on an almost fairy-tale atmosphere.

The presence of the Jews in Holland and, in particular, in Amsterdam, goes back to the second half of the 16th century. Most of them came here from Portugal. The long and bloody persecution of the Jews throughout the Iberian peninsula, especially in Spain, had caused their dispersion from the early

Some interesting views of the Magere Brug *and surrounding* buildings *by night.*

Above, the interior and exterior of the Portuguese Synagogue; *below left,* Anne Frank's house; *below right, the Synagogue which today houses the* Jewish Museum.

15th century on. Some of them had sought an escape by converting to Catholicism, but despite the fact that a few of the converts were notorious for their spiteful behavior towards their brethren, most of these new Catholics, known as Marranos, had secretly kept alive their strong Jewish feeling. During 1481-1495, the Spanish Inquisition enacted still another bitter persecution against the Jews who found temporary refuge in Portugal. But in 1536 when the Inquisition was instituted in Portugal as well, the Marranos were forced to take flight once more. Luckily, Charles V granted them the right to settle in the Netherlands where, apart from a brief period of persecution instigated by the same Inquisition, they were able to benefit from the great tolerance following the Reformation and the success of the Union of Utrecht. The converts could thus rid themselves of their falsely-acquired Catholicism and return to the faith of their forefathers. Naturally, their origins were reflected in their houses of worship. The **Portuguese Synagogue** is one of the most beautiful in the

Some scenes of the flower market which is held along the banks of the Singelgracht.

world; the vast building, the southeast façade of which faces toward Jerusalem, was erected between 1671 and 1675 by Elias Bouman and was restored in 1955. The interior consists of a single large hall, with three wooden barrel-vault ceilings, all the same size and held up by four Ionic columns. The **Anne Frank's House** is at No. 263 Prinsengracht. This young Jewish girl wrote the celebrated "Diary of Anne Frank" (called in Dutch "Het Achterhuis"), which was published in 1947. She hid in this house with her family and other Jews from July 8, 1942 to August 4, 1944, when their secret refuge was discovered and all the people in it arrested and deported.
Anne Frank, taken to the concentration camp of Bergen-Belsen, died in March 1945, only two months before the lib-

Above, the Stedelijk Museum *and the* Rijksmuseum Vincent van Gogh. *Center and below, two halls in the* Rijksmuseum Vincent van Gogh.

eration of Holland. The house today contains a thorough documentation of the deportation program carried out by the Germans against the Dutch and is visited by a continual stream of people who will not, cannot or feel they should never forget the significance of Anne Frank's story.

A huge zone on the left bank of the **Singel**, the outermost of the original circles surrounding the city, contains the complex of Amsterdam's museums. Alongside the city's other great museum, the **Stedelijk Museum**, dedicated to the history and iconography of the city and of modern art, stands the modern building which the citizens of Amsterdam have dedicated to **Van Gogh**, the painter who committed suicide in 1890. The museum contains all the paintings and drawings which were exhibited in the Stedelijk while they were still the property of his heirs. The 95 canvases and 144 drawings were then left to the museum by a descendant of van Gogh. This museum is also well-known as a center of activity in the art world.

Just beyond the Vincent van Gogh Museum we find Holland's best known art museum: the **Rijksmuseum**. In 1808 the King of Holland, Louis Bonaparte, placed on the throne by his brother, the Emperor Napoleon, decided to make Amsterdam not only the political but also the cultural capital of his kingdom. This was when the Town Hall on the Dam became the Royal Palace, and the king also created a royal art museum with its collections housed in several rooms of the palace's first floor. When Napoleon had the Kingdom of Holland incorporated into France, this became the Dutch Museum, which due to certain vicissitudes was never transferred elsewhere as planned. Then the new king, William I of the House of Orange, came to the throne, and he directed that the collections (which in the meantime had grown both in quantity and in quality) should remain in Amsterdam and that the museum should be called the Rijksmuseum van Schilderijen, or Museum of the Kingdom of the Netherlands. The works were later transferred

Vincent van Gogh,
The Clogs *and*
Self-portrait
(Rijksmuseum
Vincent van Gogh).

Vincent van Gogh, **Landscape, Fishing Boats on the Beach** (Rijksmuseum Vincent van Gogh).

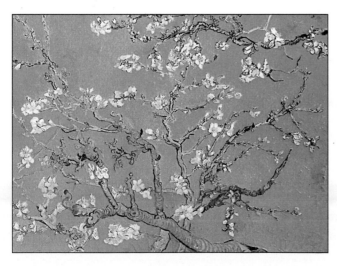

Vincent van Gogh, **The Yellow House** (Rijksmuseum Vincent van Gogh).

Vincent van Gogh, **Gaugin's Chair** (Rijksmuseum Vincent van Gogh).

Vincent van Gogh, **Almond Tree in Bloom** (Rijksmuseum Vincent van Gogh).

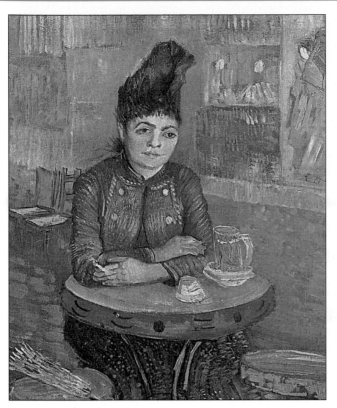

Vincent van Gogh,
**Woman at a Table
in the "Café du Tambourin"**
(Rijksmuseum Vincent van Gogh).

Vincent van Gogh,
Still life with Bottle and Lemons
(Rijksmuseum Vincent van Gogh).

Vincent van Gogh, **Self-portrait
with Straw Hat** *(Rijksmuseum
Vincent van Gogh),*

**Beach scene with Figures
and Boa**t *(Stedelijk Museum).*

The Rijksmuseum.

to the Trippenhuis, an aristocratic dwelling built between 1660 and 1664 by the rich Tripp brothers, where the museum was opened to the public in February 1817. It remained here for about seventy years, although space problems became more and more serious as the number of works it possessed continued to grow. In 1862 a competition was announced for the design of a new museum building, and 21 architects took part. Only ten years later the design submitted by P. J. H. Cuypers was accepted, and on 13 July 1885 the Rijksmuseum of Amsterdam, a grandiose building made from red brick in the neo-Gothic style, was officially opened. It has more than 260 rooms, containing not only masterpieces of painting but also superb prints, furniture, ceramics and other works of art.

The major "attraction" of the museum is of course Rembrandt van Rijn's **Night Watch**. This painting, one of his masterpieces and indeed a masterpiece of Western culture was completed by the painter when he was 36 in 1642. The large canvas (measuring 4.38 by 3.59 meters, or about 14' x 10') was commissioned to celebrate the visit of Maria de' Medici to the city. Rembrandt painted the company of Captain Frans Cocq and his lieutenant Willem van Ruytenburch, a volunteer militia group, before the march. The name by which the painting is now universally known was given to it in the 18th century when, because of oxidation of the paint, the canvas came to acquire a "nocturnal" appearance. Rembrandt broke decisively with the then fashionable tradition of group portraits and placed the figures in his painting in dramatic poses. Rembrandt, one of the greatest artists of all times, left a lasting imprint in the history of painting, drawing and engraving. Born in Leyden in 1606 to a bourgeois family, as a young man he enrolled in the local university to study humanities, but he soon left his studies and devoted himself exclusively to art. After training for several years in Leyden and Amsterdam, he decided to move to Amsterdam for good in 1631. His "Anatomy Lesson of Dr. Tulp" of 1632 brought him almost overnight fame. Contended as a portrait painter, he turned out a number of fine portraits during the period between 1636 and 1642, which was when his fame reached its highpoint. At the same time, however, his style was undergoing change and innovations were gradually being brought in. His brushwork grew broader and fuller and his palette, based on deep reds and browns with gold highlights, was becoming warmer and richer. The year 1642 was a turning point in Rembrandt's life. Deeply affected by deaths in his family, he started to change his style once more, whereupon he was able to attain an inner profundity which bestowed intensely dramatic and spiritual overtones to his painting. Throughout this period Rembrandt and his wife Saskia lived in a charming dwelling located on Sint Anthoniesbreestraat. Turned into a museum in 1911, the **house** still preserves the atmosphere of when the master lived and worked in it. This period (1642-1655), although the least happy for Rembrandt from a personal standpoint, was his finest from an artistic one. From 1655 onwards, no longer understood and sought out by his contemporaries, he fell into great poverty so that in 1656 he was forced to sell all his earthly possessions. He earned a living in partnership with his son Titus as a small-scale art dealer. The death of Titus in 1668 was the final blow dealt to this unique artist. Rembrandt died here in 1669.

*Rembrandt van Rijn, **The magistrates** (Rijksmuseum).*

*Rembrandt van Rijn, **Self-portrait**
(Rijksmuseum).*

Rembrandt van Rijn, **Night Watch**
(Rijksmuseum).

Jan Vermeer, **Girl reading a Letter**
(Rijksmuseum).

Jan Vermeer, **Woman pouring milk**
(Rijksmuseum).

From top to bottom: view of the Herengracht, *the* Munttoren, *the former* Post Office *building, the* Montelbaanstoren, *the* monument to Queen Wilhelmina, Rembrandt's house.

The Spaarndam dam *and the* monument to Pieter, *the courageous boy who saved Haarlem.*

SPAARNDAM

Spaarndam commemorates the charming legend of Pieter and the dyke. Situated a kilometer and a half northeast of Haarlem, Spaarndam is where, in 1960, Princess Irene officiated at the ceremony inaugurating a monument to the courage, selflessness and dedication Dutch youth have displayed over the centuries. The statue depicts the famous boy who, one day, while he was out taking a stroll, noticed a breach in one of the dykes. He realized that if it got any larger, it would have meant the destruction of the protective wall and thus the destruction of Haarlem itself. **Pieter** did not hesitate one moment – he stuck his finger into the hole and kept it there all night until help arrived. Unfortunately, in the meantime Pieter died, but his fearless sacrifice had avoided a catastrophe for his native city.

BREDERODE CASTLE

There are few places in Holland which can equal the charm of the Brederode Castle with its picturesque ruins salvaged from the sand dunes. Founded in the 13th century and rebuilt in the 15th, it was later enlarged in the 1500s. Its name is linked to a noble family, the de Brederodes, many of whom are well-known figures. Francis de Brederode (1465-1490), who died at the age of 25 from wounds inflicted during a battle in which the Dutch were defeated by Maximilian of Austria's troops and Henry de Brederode, who in 1566 presented the famous document signed by the Union of Nobles to the regent Margaret of Parma in Brussels, are two of historical note. The castle walls, which were unearthed in 1862 and then expertly restored, may today be admired in all their splendor. Two towers, one of which was a watchtower, the brick fortification walls and the moat have all been brought back to light.

The Brederode castle.

The Stadhuis.

HAARLEM

From the chronicles we learn that Haarlem had obtained municipal rights by the 10th century; fortified in the second half of the 12th, it became the residence of the Counts of Holland. The city did not have an easy time of it: in addition to the traditional battle that the local population was compelled to wage against the enemy from without, the sea, Haarlem was also plagued with other disasters within (three fires, one in 1155, another in 1346, and a third in 1351, and wars). Then, during the Protestant revolt of 1572 the city was subjected to a seven month long siege (lasting from December 11, 1572 to July 13, 1573) conducted by the son of the Duke of Alba, Don Frederick. Equally memorable for its duration and its tragic and glorious episodes, the outcome was terrible. Throughout the long 1572 winter the city stood fast, expecting aid from William the Silent, and was in some way able to resist the whole time, despite the unbearable hunger. When the Spaniards assassinated William, destroyed his fleet, and wiped out the armada which was supposed to be bringing help, the citizens of Haarlem were compelled to surrender, though they hoped that an honor-

Two views of the Grote Markt, *the monument to L. J. Coster, the inventor of the printing press, facing the Grote Kerk.*

able peace could be reached. But this was not to be the case: the Duke of Alba made the city pay for the seven months of siege he had been forced to conduct and the enormous death toll his troops had suffered and ordered that 1800 survivors of Haarlem be cruelly massacred. The city, though, could not be kept down and when in 1577 the army of the States General was garrisoned here, it embarked on a period of great prosperity. In the 17th century the city's splendor was enhanced by the presence of a group of painters who had either been born in or had taken up resi-

dence in Haarlem, the best-known of whom were Frans Hals and Jacob van Ruysdael. In 1862 Haarlem proudly inaugurated a museum dedicated to its most famous native son, Frans Hals which, in 1913, was moved to its present location, the Oudemannehuis. This old building had originally been erected by Lieven de Key in 1608 as an old age home, and it was where Hals himself had died. In the 17th century too, in 1636 to be exact, the tulip growing industry was born in Haarlem During April and May, the fields of "bloemenvelden" stretching south of the city afford one of the most incredible spectacles one can imagine. In addition to this marvel of nature, Haarlem also boasts a number of remarkable architectural monuments. The foremost is the **Stadhuis**, once residence of the Counts of Holland which, despite an erroneous tradition dating it in the 13th century, was erected in the middle of the 16th century and completed by Lieven de Key in the period 1620-1630. The historical section of Haarlem, the **Grote Markt**, is dominated by an imposing church, the **Grote Kerk**, better known as the Cathedral of St. Bavo. It was built in the Brabantine late Gothic style on the site of a smaller building destroyed in a fire in 1328. Inside there is an extraordinary organ with a triple keyboard, 68 registers, and 5000 pipes, built in 1738 by Christian Müller. The organ case decoration was designed by Daniel Marot. Among the people who have

Three views of the Grote Kerk *and the interior.*

*Details of the Grote Kerk: the organ,
the carved wooden pulpit (1679)
and a stained glass window.
The Amsterdamse Poort.
At the side: the Vleeshal and a detail
of the roof. On the following pages:
two views of a drawbridge, the
Teijlers Museum and a detail of the
museum's façade.*

played this organ are Mozart, Handel, and Dr. Albert
Schweitzer. The **Vleeshal** (or Vishal) is a charming contrast
to the cathedral. The old meat market is housed in a red
brick and stone building erected by Lieven de Key between
1602 and 1623 after the Renaissance style. A taste of Haarlem's glorious military past can be had at the **Amsterdamse
Poort**, the imposing remains of the 15th century walls
which once encircled the city. Extant today is a sturdy
square tower flanked by two smaller octagonal towers, in
front of which protrudes a structure with round turrets. One
more interesting historical tidbit about this city so rich in history: here in the first half of the 15th century **Laurens Jan-
szoon Coster** invented a printing press before Gutenberg's
invention in Germany.

The castle of Muiden, or Muiderslot.

MUIDERSLOT

Muiderslot, which means castle of Muiden, is reached by crossing the river Vecht at its mouth on the IJsselmeer where the tiny harbor of Muiden is located. On the site of the castle originally stood a wooden house which, from the 10th century onward, served as a toll office for ships passing through. Founded in 1205 by the Bishop of Utrecht, the castle was enlarged again and again, especially under Count Floris V who was murdered here in 1296. It was remodeled in the 15th century by Ludwig of Monfoort, During the 17th century, one of Holland's best loved poets, P. C. Hooft, lived in the castle. Today from the outside it looks like a sturdy brick cube with round towers at each corner. Inside there is a museum of history exhibiting tapestries, carpets, arms and armor, and furniture dating from the first half of the 17th century. One of the loveliest and most famous of these tapestries is the one depicting the encounter of Alexander the Great and the mother, wife, and daughters of Darius III after the battle of Isso, which was woven in Flanders in the 15th century.

ZAANDAM

The village of Zaandam, renowned for its great shipyards, has witnessed a number of historical events. One of the best-known is the visit paid by Peter the Great, Czar of Russia, in 1697. The young monarch was at the time travelling under a false name, Peter Michailov, and working as a common laborer in the shipyards so he could study shipbuilding techniques. Despite this disguise, his real identity was soon discovered by the local population and he was compelled to flee Zaandam and seek refuge in Amsterdam. The **home** in which Peter lived during his brief stay was donated to Czar Nicholas II, who had it restored and turned into a museum. Near the town of Zaandam is another noteworthy sight.

Zaanse Schans

The picturesque village of Zaanse Schans is situated near Zaandam. The village, which stands along the banks of the river Zaan, is an exact reproduction of the typical landscape of the polders of North Holland. The small rural center consists of green-painted wooden houses and windmills dating back to the XVII-XIX centuries. These buildings have been faithfully reconstructed at Zaanse Schans, although some of them come from other locations in Holland. From the car park leading to this open-air museum, visitors walk along the only street in the village discovering, along the way, various buildings housing small collections of local art and various types of craft and manufacturing activities: the Catharina Hoeve cheese factory, the In de Gekroonde Duyvekater bakery-museum, the Het Jagerhuis antiques and curiosities shop, the Aan't Glop art gallery, the **Het Noordenhuis** museum (originally the home of a Zaandijk merchant, 1670), the typical De Hoop Op d'Swarte Walvis restaurant, the Albert Heijn shop-museum, the **clock and watch museum**, the shipyard and the clog factory, where it is pos-

The Czar Peter Huisje *(the house of Peter the Great) and two halls of the museum inside. Below, a view of* Zaanse Schans.

The Het Noordenhuis museum *and a detail of the façade (top), the* Mill Museum *(center), the* De Hadel mill *(below).*

sible to buy custom-made examples of this typical Dutch footwear. The seven mills built here are very interesting and some of them are still in working order: the **De Hadel** mill, originally from Midwoud, the mill for producing De Huisman mustard, the **De Gekroonde Poelenburg** sawmill, the mill for manufacturing colors **De Kat**, the **De Zoeker** and De Bonte Hen oil mills, and the De Windhond mill.

The De Zoeker *mill and two details of the internal mechanism (top), the* De Gekroonde Poelenburg *sawmill (center), two details of the internal mechanism of the* De Kat *mill (below).*

Some stages of clog manufacture in the Zaanse Schans factory.

CLOGS

Clogs were invented in the late Middle Ages and, in the past, were worn in all the countries of Northern Europe. This type of footwear is still very widespread in Holland, albeit not as much as in the past. The popularity of clogs stems from the fact that they are practical and simple to wear. Their shape protects the feet from the muddy ground which characterizes the Dutch countryside below sea level, and they are easy to put on since they have no laces.

Today, around three million pairs of clogs a year are produced in the Netherlands, mostly destined for the tourist market. Alongside the industrial production, where each manufacturing phase is almost totally automated, a clog-making cottage industry still survives, often supplying high level products and keeping alive a tradition of ancient origins.

At one time, clog manufacture was an activity linked to the rural world. In the time they had free from their work in the fields, the peasants used to make clogs for their own personal use. This resulted in a variety of shapes and decorations, which varied according to the occasion for which the clog was created. There were clogs for everyday wear, for parties, for weddings, for children and even for infants. Each Dutch region had its own special clog shapes thanks to the specialization of the local craftsmen. Only from 1920 onwards when electrical machinery was introduced, has the production of clogs been automated in order to meet the growing demands of the mass market.

Originally, clogs were only made from willow. This was subsequently replaced by wood from the Canadian poplars which today characterize the landscape of many Dutch regions. Only a few craftsmen still use willow for their products. In order to make a pair of clogs, the craftsman uses a considerable number of blades and knives for first cutting, then hollowing out and finally shaping the wood. This is a very precise process since the left clog must be perfectly symmetrical to the right one. The final touch is the pictorial decoration or carving of the clogs, which can reach levels of incredible virtuosity with the creation of unique articles.

The national clog fair is held every year at St. Oedenrode, in

Some of the numerous multi-colored pairs of clogs displayed in the Zaanse Schans factory.

Brabant. On this occasion, the best craftsmen and factories of Holland compete for the "Best clog of the year" award. During the fair, clogs of all types and shapes are displayed, demonstrating that this tradition is still alive, thanks to the perfect integration of craft production and machine manufacturing: the handmade model is still held as an example for industrial production.

A typical house *in Broek in Waterland. Below,
the* Grote Kerk *and an interior view of the church.*

On the following page: detail of the Speeltoren
in Monnickendam, the Waag building with the
Speeltoren in the background, the Grote Kerk
and an interior view of the church.

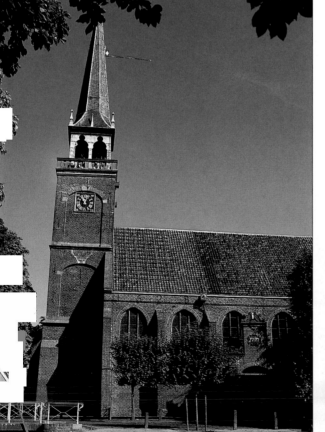

BROEK IN WATERLAND

This charming village is made up of small houses with characteristic painted tile roofs. Each house has a little garden decorated with delightful flower arrangements. According to an ancient local tradition, it was only possible to enter a property after taking one's shoes off. Even the French Emperor Napoleon I was forced to present himself to the mayor in stockinged feet when he passed through the small town. The **Reformed Church**, in the center of the town, was rebuilt in 1648. Inside, there is a beautiful carved wooden pulpit onto which the light filtering through the XVIIIth century stained-glass windows shines.

MONNICKENDAM

The main attraction of this pleasant port is the **Speeltoren**, the clock-tower (1591) which faces onto the Nordeinde, the main street of Monnickendam. As each hour strikes, a carillon of bells starts up and the small animated wooden figurines, with their mechanical dance, peep out of the small rectangular window below the tower's terrace. Next to the tower is the **Waag**, the ancient weighing station (1660) with its elegant classical lines. The imposing tower, alongside the late Gothic **Grote Kerk** (XVIth century), dominates the town center. The interior of the church has two aisles divided by columns and crowned by a remarkable keel-shaped wooden ceiling.

The port *of Marken and two views of the interior of a* typical fisherman's home.

The port *of Volendam.*

VOLENDAM AND MARKEN

These charming ports have managed to preserve their ancient character like few other Dutch cities. **Volendam** is famous for the handsome native costume worn by the local inhabitants. These may be admired in the morning hours when the women are on their way to church (the population is mostly Catholic). The women wear pleated blue or black striped jackets over a seven-colored skirt called a "zevenkleurige rok". Extremely picturesque is their head-gear hiding practically all of the face, and looking like some kind of medieval helmet. The men wear short fitted jackets trimmed with silver buttons, flaring black pants and round hats. In **Marken** the little wooden houses painted in bright colors and, needless to say, all spotlessly clean, look like ships. Their tiny interiors are incredibly but neatly crammed with objects. The inhabitants, mostly Protestants, are mainly fishermen and wear their native dress every day, just as many Dutch people do. The women sport red jackets over colored bodices and wear coits on their heads. The men wear jackets over loose-fitting trousers, tied at the knee and black stockings. Both sexes have the typical "klompen", i.e. wooden clogs, on their feet, a charming reminder of the time when Holland was still a primarily agricultural country.

TRADITIONAL DUTCH COSTUMES

*I*n the past, each Dutch region had its own typical costumes, which have today been replaced by modern clothes. The custom of dressing in traditional style still survives in just a few towns, mainly on the occasion of local festivals. The white lace bonnet is the most typical element of the countrywoman's clothing, especially on special holidays. The Protestant women usually wear a shell-shaped bonnet, whereas the Catholic women's bonnet is shaped like a trapezoid, with another light blue bonnet worn underneath. The Catholic women's clothing is usually lively and colorful. Their wide skirts are often covered with an apron or a shawl, in various styles, with decorative patterns which vary according to the region. On top of their long- or short-sleeved blouses or bodices, the Dutch women often wear delightful jackets. Their jewelry is limited to simple gold earrings and necklaces made from coral or other precious materials, but always of a very frugal appearance. One typical adornment is a gold band, worn in the hair, which has oval-shaped ends protruding from the sides of the bonnet. The traditional festival clothing for men is marked by baggy pants or breeches, usually black, and very tight-fitting jackets, adorned with silver buttons. When they are wearing their traditional costumes, both men and women also wear the inevitable clogs.

The Stadhuis *and the* Museum *of Edam, two typical* drawbridges *and a* room of the museum.

EDAM

This pleasant little town, founded in the XIIth century, is today one of the major dairy producing and trading centers in Holland. The **Stadhuis**, the 18th century town hall built in 1737, overlooks the main square of Edam, the Damplein. On the opposite side of the square is the **Edams Museum**, housed in a late Gothic building dated 1540. The city-museum hosts collections of paintings, pottery, engravings, prints and important documents concerning local history.

The slender structure of the Speeltoren, the ancient bell-tower of the Church of Our Lady (XVth century), now destroyed, dominates the city center. Inside the Speeltoren is a carillon built by Peter van den Ghein in 1562. Edam is also rightfully famous for its typical white-painted wooden **drawbridges**, which are still used today to cross the numerous canals traversing the city.

However, Edam's fame is linked above all to the cheese which bears its name: Edammerkaas, famous throughout the world. The **Kaasmarkt** is held every

Some images of the lively Kaasmarkt *in Edam.*

Wednesday morning during the summer months: this is a lively open-air cheese market during which large crowds of buyers cram into the city squares to appraise and buy this much appreciated local product. Edam's cheese market is second in importance only to the one held in Alkmaar.

The Waag; a distinctive drawbridge *in Alkmaar, the apse of the* Grote Kerk, *cheeses displayed in front of the Waag during the* cheese market.

ALKMAAR

Cited in a chronicle of the year 800 as Almere, Alkmaar was long a stronghold during the defense waged by the Dutch against the Frisian invaders. Then, besieged in 1573 by Don Federico of Toledo (brother of the Duke of Alba), it was the first Dutch city to withstand the assault of the Spanish troops who were forced to break off their siege and retreat. The city is renowned for its **cheese market**, the most important in Holland, which is held every Friday in the summer months at 10 a.m. before the public **weighing station**. The building was originally a chapel consecrated to the Holy

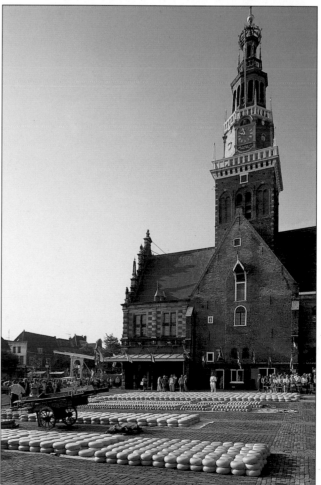

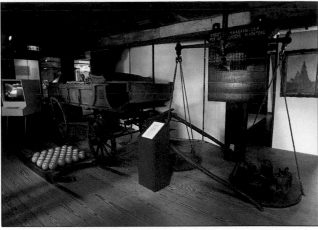

Spirit (built in 1386 in the Gothic style, it was later rebuilt in 1582). Pieter Cornelisz designed the bell-tower which was erected between 1595 and 1599. On top is a carillon with horsemen figures by Melchior de Haze (1688).

The round cheeses, weighing anywhere from 2 to 6 kilos, are either yellow (for domestic consumption) or red (for export). The cheeses are transported to the marketplace on huge flat-bottomed barges from which they are tossed to the cheese porters waiting nearby with their gondola-shaped wooden barrows. The porters belong to an old guild which has been granted the exclusive privilege of transporting the cheeses. A "father" supervises teams of 28 porters further divided into 4 sub-groups known as "veems." The veems may be distinguished by the blue, red, green or yellow ribbon on each porter's straw hat. The task of the porters is to load the cheeses upon special planks which hold at least 80 2-kilo cheeses. They then take them over to the public weighing bridge where the quotations are chalked up on special blackboards. The team that totals the most is awarded the title "guild leader group" and holds the title until market day of the following week. At the end of the market day, the porters all go to drink special beer prepared for the occasion which is served up in special pewter mugs handed down from generation to generation for centuries. This is how cheese has been marketed for the last three hundred years in Alkmaar.

Some of the objects displayed in the Kaasmuseum *and some images of the* cheese market *which is held every Friday morning in Alkmaar, from mid April to mid September.*

Windmills *along the road between Alkmaar and Hoorn. The* Oosterpoort *in Hoorn, the* monument to J. P. Coen *on the Rode Steen, with the* Waag *on the left.*

HOORN

The city was called Hoorn after the horn shape of its port. The horn of plenty is in fact the symbol of the city and we find it carved upon the façades of houses and on the crests of palaces, and painted upon the flags of ships. Already mentioned in 14th century manuscripts, Hoorn grew rapidly. It flourished throughout the 15th century, reaching its height of splendor in the 17th century. It was the birthplace of several great men. The explorer Willem Schouten, the first European to sail around the tip of the South American continent (which he named Hoorn after his native town though it is now called Cape Horn); Abel Tasman, who discovered New Zealand and Tasmania; Jan Pieterzoon Coen who founded Batavia (present-day Jakarta) in Java and who was governor of the island from 1618 to 1629; and Bontekoe, another celebrated explorer of the far-off Indies, who lived in the 17th century, are among the best-known. As was the case for numerous other cities on the Zuiderzee, Hoorn's decline began in the 18th century when the supremacy of the Dutch fleet was overshadowed by the English merchant marine on the great international trade routes. But numerous reminders of Hoorn's past splendor such as the Bos- suhuizen (Bossu House), at the end of the Grote Oost are still extant. The Bossuhuizen was named after the Spanish Admiral defeated and taken prisoner aboard his own galleon "The Inquisition" on October 11, 1753 in the vicinity of Cape Horn by the fleets of the cities of Hoorn, Edam, Enkhuizen and Monnikendam. The highlights of this battle are illustrated in the sculpture and inscriptions decorating the façade of the house with the winds personified by two figures of nude women.

The monument to the Cabin Boys of Bontekoe in the port of Hoorn. The Hoofdtoren *and a detail of the tower coping.*

ENKHUIZEN

Once a port on the Zuiderzee, Enkhuizen today is a flourishing tulip growing center. It reached the height of its glory in the 17th century when it could boast over 40,000 inhabitants and a fishing fleet of over 400 vessels. Herring fishing brought prosperity to the shipowners who, during the early years of the 17th century, were able to get even richer from the lucrative trade they carried on with the East Indies. Then when the port was filled in (at the time the north dyke was being built), thus blocking off any outlet to the sea,

Enkhuizen started on a slow, but inevitable decline, the end result of which was that the city eventually became a charming city-museum. Museum too is the Peperhuis, or Spice House, once the biggest warehouse belonging to the East India Company. Inside are objects and documents which give an idea of the architecture, furnishings, dress, and everyday articles of the whole surrounding region. Enkhuizen is particularly known for the Zuider Spui, a charming group of fishermen's houses with quaint slanted fronts. Noteworthy are the striking sculpted façade decorations of the Weeshuis (or Orphanage), dated 1616, and the sturdy **Drommedaris**, a two-part tower built at the entrance to the old port as part of the city fortifications in 1540. The 16th century carillon on top is famous as the most beautiful in all of Holland.

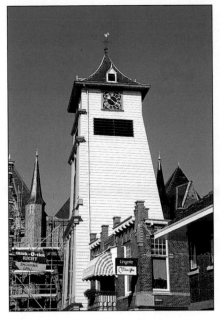

Above, the Gomarustoren, *the* Weeshuis; *below, the* Drommedaris tower, *a* 17th century house, *the bell-tower of the* Zuiderkerk; *below, an* aerial view *of the city.*

The three chimneys of the Akersloot furnaces *and some scenes of the* fishermen's village *(Zuiderzee Museum).*

Zuiderzee Museum

The Zuiderzee Museum in Enkhuizen consists of an indoor (**Binnenmuseum**) and an outdoor museum (**Buitenmuseum**). The first is located in the Peperhuis, or Spice House, built in 1625, which was once the biggest warehouse of the East India Company. Today, it contains objects and documents illustrating the customs, costumes, furnishings and architecture of the towns overlooking the Zuiderzee, before it was blocked off following the construction of the Afsluitdijk dyke, which was completed in 1932. The second is located along the banks of the IJsselmeer, north of Enkhuizen. The open-air part of the Zuiderzee Museum consists of around 130 buildings from 42 different locations which have been rebuilt here. The Museum can be reached by land or by sea, with craft leaving Enkhuizen every 15 minutes. The Buitenmuseum buildings are divided into districts, each marked with the name of the town used as a

The interior of the shipyard, *the* polder, *two scenes of the* fishermen's village *(Zuiderzee Museum).*

model for its construction. The interiors of the dwellings faithfully reproduce the everyday environment of the people who used to live there. Some buildings house permanent exhibitions illustrating various aspects of the history of Zuiderzee from the last century up until 1932.

The Kasteel Radboud, *the halls inside the castle, the* De Herder *mill.*

MEDEMBLIK

Medemblik, one of the oldest settlements in North Holland, is one of the many "dead cities" to be found in the vicinity of the Zuiderzee. It was, in fact, the capital of the Frisians even before Hoorn and Enkhuizen ever existed, since, according to tradition, it was founded in 334 A.D. Traces of Medemblik's long ago prosperity are still visible in the warehouses, churches, and dwellings which are living proof of that past glory, later followed by a lengthy unbroken period of silent abandon in the 1700s.

Reaching Medemblik by way of Enkhuizen, the first building one notes south of the city is the **castle of Radboud**, named after a Frisian king who lived in the 8th century A.D. This stronghold, typically medieval in appearance, was rebuilt by Count Floris V in 1288. Partially ruined and demolished in the 17th and 18th centuries, it is nevertheless still an imposing sight with its timeworn bricks and slate roof, rising at the entrance to the harbor.

AFSLUITDIJK

This dyke (literally, the closing dyke) holds an essential place in the centuries long, highly dramatic struggle Holland has been waging against the sea. Starting from the 17th century, various ways to separate the Zuiderzee from the North Sea were discussed. Actually the earliest plan dates back to 1667, but the ensuing difficulties always seemed too great to be overcome and no action was ever taken. Then after the catastrophic floods of 1916 it was decided to erect a dyke which, by uniting the provinces of North Holland to Friesland, would serve a dual purpose: it would prevent floods from devastating land in the vicinity while at the same time new territory could be reclaimed from the terrible North Sea.

Designed by Cornelis Lely in 1892, the dyke was begun in 1919 and inaugurated on May 28, 1932: 30 kilometers long and 90 meters wide, it stands 7 meters above mean sea level. 23 million cubic meters of sand, 13 million cubic meters of clay filler and 1 million blocks for paving the slope were required in its construction. At either end of the dyke, locks regulate navigation of the IJsselmeer, the semi-freshwater lake formed by the closing off of the Zuiderzee. Its total depth is 3.5 meters. At the beginning of the dyke, which is surmounted by a four-lane motorway, there is a monument to Cornelis Lely, while upon another monument further along there is an inscription which reads, "A living people builds its future."

The motorway which runs along the edge of the Afsluitdijk.

TEXEL

The island of Texel is the biggest and southernmost of the Frisian Islands, located near the coast, a 20 minute ferry ride away from Den Helder, 80 kilometers north of Amsterdam. The island covers a surface area of 18,335 hectares (it is 24 kilometers long and 9 wide). The western coast is constantly battered by strong winds and characterized by an interminable light-colored, fine sandy beach, which is one of the longest and most beautiful in Europe. Originally, the island of Texel was a large estate annexed by the Counts of Holland in 1183. Today, the island's seven villages are inhabited by little over 12,000 people, mainly fishermen and sheep breeders. Another important economical resource is ecological tourism, thanks to the 19 nature reserves scattered throughout the island of Texel, where 300 different species of birds build their nests. Some of these reserves are open to bird-watching enthusiasts, who come to visit from all over the world. A prudent policy of protection and exploitation has resulted in the naturalistic oases of the island of Texel offering a truly unique panorama of birds whose natural habitat is a damp, seaside environment. The most famous reserve is **De Eijerlandse Duinen** (or "dunes of the land of eggs"), situated on the southernmost point of the island.

A view of De Koog, *three glimpses of the* De Muy *reserve: an expanse of* willow-herb, *the* dunes *seen from the observatory, a* typical house.

Numerous species of birds can be observed among the sand dunes: curlews, eider ducks, herring gulls, common gulls, lapwings, sheldrakes and some pairs of the rare marsh owl. In the **De Muy** reserve, around a small lake in the middle of the dunes, in addition to a substantial colony of herons, spoonbills can be found, birds which only nest in two other places in western Europe: the Guadalquivir delta in Spain, and Lake Neusiedl, in Austria. The **De Slufter** reserve, a sea water canal, hosts a colony of wading birds. Here it is

Above, two views from the De Slufter *reserve observatory. Below, the* Vuurtoren lighthouse, the old De Bol mill, *the Lancasterdijk* Wad *(expanse of sand and silt) at low tide.*

possible to observe avocets and godwits rummaging in the slime with their long beaks. Finally, the De Westerduinen reserve hosts a noisy colony of herring gulls and is also a nesting site for oyster-catchers.

*Some of the numerous species of birds found
on the island of Texel: 1. and 5. gray herons, 2. avocets,
3. common terns, 4. lesser black-backed gulls,
6. lapwings, 7. great crested grebes,
8. oyster-catchers, 9. black-headed gulls.
Below, a colony of gulls in the coastal
area of the De Slufter reserve.*

LEYDEN

Leyden may be defined as the most intellectual city of the realm, not only because of its celebrated university, but also for its group of philosophers and scientists who rapidly brought the university to a high European standard. The city grew up along the main branch of the Rhine River: recent excavations have established that by 800 a settlement already existed on the spot. Its Roman name was "Lugdunum Batavorum." Shortly after the year 800, the Danish king Harold erected a keep here which would be taken over, a hundred years later, by the Counts of Holland. Under the reign of the Counts, the city, then known as "Leithen," expanded and took up trade and commerce, so that by the beginning of the 13th century, it was granted municipal rights. Leyden has become a part of Dutch legend for a memorable historical event. From October 31, 1573 it was besieged by General Valdez, commander of the Spanish troops, who was hoping to conquer the city by starving it into surrender, but after a year had gone by, Leyden was still valorously resisting. The local paupers and beggars, called "gueux," thought up the idea of bringing aid and reinforcement to the besieged city by opening a dike every night, and thus allowing the Dutch fleet, which traveled from one lake to another, to reach Leyden in no time. On October 3, 1574 the siege was lifted and the gueux, thereafter known as "watergeuzen," i.e. water paupers, were able to distribute herring and white bread to the famished city. The episode has become a tradition: on October 3 of every year the Burgomaster distributes the same simple food to the citizens of Leyden so that everyone may remember those formidable days of heroism. Moreover, the history of the university is linked to the very same episode. In order to express his gratitude to the city for the tenacity and courage displayed throughout the long siege, William of Orange proposed a choice of one or two benefits: either the city could be exempted from paying taxes forever or else be granted its own university. Leyden opted for the latter solution and the following year was endowed with its university campus which from then on became the focal point of the whole town. It was on account of the university that Leyden became the crossroads and meeting place of the intelligentsia of all of Europe. The greatest minds of the 16th and 17th centuries taught in it. We shall briefly mention: the mathematician Snellius, the jurist Hugo de Groot, the physician Boerhaave (of whom it was said the address "Boerhaave, Europe" was more than enough for the couriers), the botanist Clasius (famous for his experiments on tulips, of which he managed to produce an incredible number of varieties), the physicist Musschenbroek (the inventor of the first condenser), and the physicist Huygens (who set forth the theory of the undulation movement of light), not to mention the philosopher Descartes. During this period, Leyden set another record in the field of cultural activity: in 1617 a printing shop specializing in rare languages such as Chinese, Arabic and Persian was founded. Nevertheless, the city's prosperity was not linked to its cultural fervor, but rather it was based upon an extremely flourishing cloth trade. Whoever loves art will certainly find Leyden a treat. The name of the painter Geerten tot Sint Jans is the first one which comes to mind, immediately followed by Lucas of Leyden. But life was not always easy for Leyden. In 1807 in the center of the attractive neighborhood known as **Rapenburg** a ship

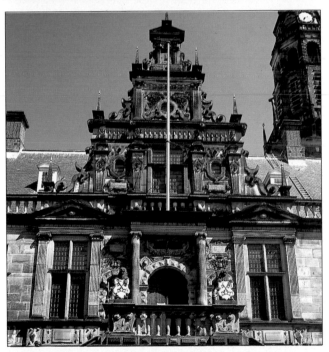

The Stadhuis *and a detail of the façade coping, the* Hooglandse Kerk.

with a cargo of gunpowder exploded and a large section was totally destroyed. This area, for a long time known as the Ruins, has been transformed into the Van der Werf Park. Nevertheless, there are still monuments which are living proof of the city's glorious past: the 17th century **Stadhuis**, destroyed in 1929 (only the façade of which designed by Lieven de Key was partially spared), the picturesque Vismarkt, the old fish market, and the quaint **Korenbeursbrug**, the bridge where wheat prices were negotiated, with its classical style wooden portico that the local inhabitants call "our own Rialto." In addition to these monuments there are the churches: the **Pieterskerk**, now Protestant, an imposing double aisled Gothic church consecrated in 1121 and the **Hooglandse Kerk**, just a tiny wooden chapel dedicated to St. Pancratius in the 14th century, and later rebuilt in the Gothic style two hundred years later. In addition to the churches there are the museums, the foremost of which is the **Rijksmuseum van Oudheden** (National Museum of Antiquities), one of the greatest archeological museums in all of Europe with its prehistoric, Etruscan, Greek, Egyptian and Roman collections. On the same level is the Rijksmuseum voor Volkenkunde (Ethnographic Museum) which was founded in 1837, thus making it one of the oldest in Europe. The objects on display are masterpieces of art from the various civilizations ranging from the Americas to Africa and the Orient. Especially noteworthy is the Indonesian collection. We must not overlook the Museum voor de Geschiedenis der Natuurwetensschappen, the National Museum of the History of Science, which contains a huge number of historical instruments and documents and the Stedelijk Museum, also known as Lakenhal, located in the cloth merchants' building, with its collections of 15th, 16th and 17th century Dutch and Flemish art.

The imposing façade of the Hooglandse Kerk, *interior and exterior views of the* Pieterskerk, *the* Gravensteen.

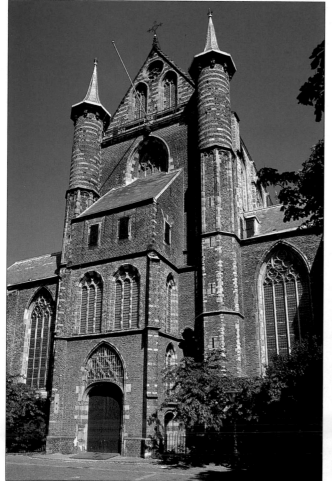

*The Corn Exchange or
Korenbeursbrug, a canal
near the building, the Marekerk
and the Marebrug, with the church
in the background.*

Two views of the canals of Leyden, the Waag en Boterhuis and a detail of the bas-relief on the façade, two vistas of the Rapenburg.

A room in the Rijksmuseum van Oudheden,
the museum entrance, the Burgsteeg *leading
to the Burcht, the* De Valk Stedelijk Molenmuseum.

Some scenes of the tulip fields which stretch as far as the eye can see around Lisse.

LISSE AND TULIPS

*T*he town of Lisse is located around 15 kilometers north of Leyden and is one of the main tulip growing centers. *Lisse is surrounded by fields of these flowers and other bulbous varieties which stretch as far as the eye can see. The Keukenhof park is located on the outskirts of the town. From mid March until the beginning of June, it is possible to admire the colorful blooming of millions of bulbous flowers in the park's hothouses and flowerbeds.*
Holland is justly famous for its cultivation of bulbous plants which cover a surface area of 17,500 hectares in the area lying behind the coast, from Katwijk to Den Helder. The introduc-

tion of tulips to the Netherlands dates back to the middle of the XVIth century. This plant, native to Turkey and central Asia, adapted well to the sandy soil of the Dutch countryside. This led to a diffusion of the cultivation of this precious flower throughout the following centuries, until it became one of the main items of the Dutch economy. In addition to tulips, a variety of other bulbous plants are cultivated in Holland today: lilies, gladioli, hyacinths, daffodils, irises and crocuses. Present production figures total around 7.5 billion bulbs per year, 51% of which are destined to be planted in gardens all over the world.

The Kurhaus *building
and two views of the crowded*
beach *at Scheveningen.*

SCHEVENINGEN

Scheveningen, actually the outskirts of The Hague, is one of the foremost resort towns of Holland (though we must not fail to mention Katwijk, Noordwijk and Zandvoort). In the 14th century it was a little fishing village; then, over 150 years ago, it was transformed into a resort. In the summer months Scheveningen is alive with thousands of tourists, many of whom come from across the German border. The **Kurhaus** (opened in 1885) is the most important establishment in town. Meeting place of the cream of the European nobility at the turn of the century, it is the major drawing card of the town. In 1961 a tremendous pier stretching 400 meters into the water was put up. It has three round buildings which contain a solarium, a restaurant, and a 46 meter tall observation tower. The beach is protected from the violent high tides of the North Sea by stone jetties placed in the water.

The Ridderzaal *in the Binnenhof courtyard;
the* neo-Gothic fountain *in front of the Ridderzaal.*

THE HAGUE

The Hague has a different name in practically every tongue, but its official name is actually 's Gravenhage which the Dutch prefer to abbreviate as Den Haag. The city is first mentioned in a document dated 1242 as "Die Haghe," or the hunting reserve of the Counts, as the counts of Holland originally had a hunting lodge in the woods which once covered the present site of the city. This early construction was thereafter transformed into a castle by William II of Holland who, once he was crowned Emperor of the Roman-Germanic Empire in 1247, was anxious to possess a residence worthy of his new title. The castle was enlarged under his son, Count Floris V and, along with the royal residence, the settlement which had meanwhile sprung up around it, started to expand. This development continued right into the 14th century when Albert of Bavaria, regent of Holland, set up his court there and the castle became the official residence of the Stathouder while the new city became the seat of the central government. In 1586 the meeting of the General States of the Netherlands, then in revolt against the Spanish dominion, was held here, but oddly enough, despite these illustrious precedents, it was not until Louis Bonaparte was made king of Holland by his brother Napoleon I, that The Hague was fully acknowledged as a major city (though the king had originally taken up resi-

The back and interior of the Ridderzaal; *two views of the* Binnenhof, *the* Grenadierspoort.

dence in Utrecht and later moved to Amsterdam). When the house of Orange rose to the throne, The Hague resumed its diplomatic importance and became a kind of headquarters for international conferences: in 1899, 1907, 1929, and 1930 important ones were held here. Still the seat of numerous international organizations, the territory of The Hague, now joined up with the suburbs of Scheveningen, reaches the coast. This is another factor which adds to the quaint charm of this city, modern in some ways, antique and aristocratic in others; it is also a garden city thanks to the number and size of the public and private parks which dot its territory. Sightseeing in The Hague is a truly unforgettable experience. The city is crammed with historical monuments, picturesque streets and corners to discover unexpectedly, as well as striking oddities. The great architectural complex of

The Mauritshuis, *two rooms inside the museum.*

the old residence of the Stathouder is today a series of build-ings and squares which serve to esthetically enliven the city center. The **Binnenhof** (literally, inner court) is wholly dom-inated by the façade of the **Ridderzaal**, or Knights' Hall, one of the loveliest works of Gothic civic architecture in the city. The building, erected by Floris V in 1280, presents a majestic triangular-shaped façade flanked by cylindrical towers. The inside consists of a single hall covered by a wooden beam ceiling. Here every year on the third Tuesday of September, called Prinsjesdag, the Queen solemnly opens the new session of Parliament by reading the Crown's state-ment to the nation. She arrives at the Ridderzaal in a gilded coach drawn by 8 horses with an escort made up of mem-bers of the various branches of the armed forces, "gromms", and soldiers clad in the livery of the House of Orange. The ceremony itself is quite solemn and dignified, but, at the same time, simple and understated. The Dutch appreciate the simplicity of their sovereign, which is one of the reasons for their longstanding affection for the members of the House of Orange. While Binnenhof means inner court, Buitenhof means outer court. This huge bustling square, now the much trafficked center of the downtown area, was originally the outer courtyard belonging to the Binnenhof. Today it provides everything that the sightseer could ever desire: department stores, banks, and famous typically

Dutch eating spots. Nearby is the **Gevangenpoort**, an old city gate to the Binnenhof. Originally built out of wood in the 13th century and later rebuilt as a prison, the building now houses a small museum of torture instruments with several exhibits of the devices used for that purpose in bygone days. It was here that Cornelis de Witt, wrongfully charged with having participated in the conspiracy which led to the assassination of the Prince of Orange, was imprisoned. When de Witt's brother, the great statesman and then Prime Minister, Jan de Witt came to the prison so that he could intercede on his brother's behalf, the citizenry, boiling with anger and hate, rose up and brutally massacred the two brothers. Today a **statue of Jan de Witt** proudly looks down at the Plaats, a huge square, once filled with old houses which were torn down to make way for the elegant boutiques now surrounding it. The pride of the city, and one of its best-known features, is the Vijver, the waterway in which many of the most beautiful monuments of the city are reflected. The most important is the **Mauritshuis**, a graceful Renaissance palace

Two views of the Parliament building, *with the Mauritshuis on the left. The* Gevangenpoort *and two rooms of the museum inside; the* monument to Jan de Witt.

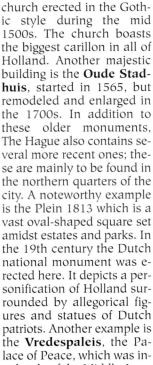

The Oude Stadhuis, *the* equestrian monument to William I the Silent, *opposite the Noordeinde Paleis; the* Het Paleis.

church erected in the Gothic style during the mid 1500s. The church boasts the biggest carillon in all of Holland. Another majestic building is the **Oude Stadhuis**, started in 1565, but remodeled and enlarged in the 1700s. In addition to these older monuments, The Hague also contains several more recent ones; these are mainly to be found in the northern quarters of the city. A noteworthy example is the Plein 1813 which is a vast oval-shaped square set amidst estates and parks. In the 19th century the Dutch national monument was erected here. It depicts a personification of Holland surrounded by allegorical figures and statues of Dutch patriots. Another example is the **Vredespaleis**, the Palace of Peace, which was inspired by the Flemish architectural style of the Middle Ages, but which was actually built between 1907 and 1913. The building was an initiative of Czar Nicholas II who was strongly in favor of holding a new world peace conference in 1898 which would once and for all put an end to the wars afflicting humanity. One of the most intriguing figures representing the Dutch Humanistic spirit is Hendrik Willem **Mesdag**, born in 1831 in Groningen. Son of a banker, he began following his father's footsteps, until, aged 35, he decided to dedicate himself wholly to painting. His decision to change his lifestyle so radically was supported by his wife, S. van Houten, who was also a painter. Husband and wife left Holland for Brussels where they studied under established artists until they returned to The Hague and Scheveningen where Mesdag could put into practice the teachings of his master, Willem Roëlofs; Roëlofs had opened his eyes to the "en plein air" style which had been championed by the French Barbizon school. While working as a painter – and he even reaped some success when a seascape of his won a prize – he also started collecting paintings, china and silver. The whole collection put together by the Mesdags, and the house bought especially to show it off, were donated to the state in 1903, with the clause that nothing could ever be added or removed. The fact that Mesdag's collection is the result of pure personal taste and nothing else makes it truly unique. Even if there are no real masterpieces in it, it still reveals the social and cultural milieu of Mesdag's time. In fact, as representative of the style of his day, he collected Dutch and French naturalistic and pre-impressionist painters, foremost of whom are Millet, Theodore Rousseau, Courbet and Daubigny.

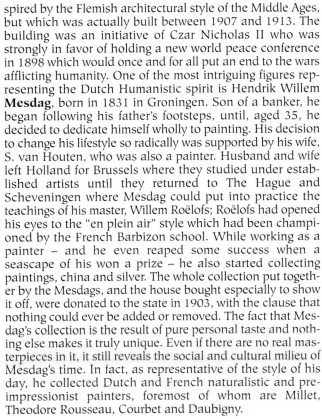

The Museon *and a room in the museum, the* Museum Mesdag, *below, the* Vredespaleis.

ROTTERDAM

Rotterdam is the second largest city in Holland and since 1968 holds the record as the world's largest **port**. This gives an idea of the city's incredible development from a settlement on the bank of the tiny Rotte River (which empties into the Maas). A dike on the Rotte is recorded for the first time in a document dated 1283. In 1340 it was granted municipal rights and ten years later its inhabitants received from the Counts of Holland the authorization to build a canal leading to Leyden and Delft which allowed them to exploit the fast-growing and lucrative commerce of English woolens. This marked the beginning of Rotterdam's growth as a commercial port. Even though the tragic effects of wars and natural disasters at times interrupted the city's economic growth (for example, the siege conducted by Maximilian of Austria in 1489, the fire of 1563, and the sacking and looting by the Spaniards in 1572), the city never ceased its bustling trade, especially with the French ports on the English Channel and the Mediterranean Sea to which it exported its fishing and agricultural products and from which it imported salt, wine, and fruit. The traffic became so heavy that after 1600, Rotterdam was compelled to build a bigger port with ten more especially wide wharves. After 1870 a new waterway, the Nieuwe Waterweg, an eighteen kilometer long, man-made canal was built; it provided faster, more direct access to the sea. This is the period when Rotterdam became a great international port and from then on its traffic has never stopped increasing. The growth was so rapid that between 1870 and 1940 twenty new

The port *of Rotterdam by night,*
three views of the Stadhuis.

Above and left: the Stadhuis *and a detail.*
Right: the Lange Jan

MIDDELBURG

Capital of the province of Zeeland, a region which for centuries was contended by the sea, the city is situated on the Isle of Walcheren and connected to the mainland. Middelburg's development had its start about 1100 around an abbey of Premonstratensian monks. The flourishing cloth trade carried on with England and the lucrative importation of French wine made Middelburg so prosperous throughout the Middle Ages that it even rivaled Bruges. In the 17th and 18th centuries the East India Company set up a great warehouse in the city and this increased its prosperity even more. In all its long history, Middelburg suffered the greatest damage when, during World War II, on May 17, 1940, fire bombs dropped by the German air force rained upon the city's major monuments, thus causing death and destruction. Nevertheless, thanks to the loving care of those who desired that they be repaired and restored, the monuments were brought back to life and today they can be enjoyed in all their splendor. On the Middelburg Markt stands what is considered the most beautiful and what is definitely the most elaborately adorned **Stadhuis** in Holland. The façade is typically Flemish, a masterpiece of the Flamboyant Gothic style. On the first level are statues depicting the counts of Zeeland and their wives. They are placed inside double niches between the windows and surmounted by finely-carved little canopies. Another unusual feature of the building is the 55 meter tall belfry with four little towers at each corner which are joined to the central one by delicate little buttresses. Middelburg's most precious jewel, however, is the huge and grandiose **Abbey** which is reached by way of a tiny square known as Balans. The complex, today the headquarters for the province's government offices, was founded in about 1100 and was occupied by the monastic order of the Premonstratensians from 1128 to 1559. The abbey actually comprises two churches, i.e. the **Nieuwe Kerk** and the Koorkerk. The former, in the Flamboyant Gothic style, has no aisles and is noteworthy for its unusual star-shaped stone vaulting. The latter, 14th century Gothic in style, houses the Nicolai organ built in Utrecht between 1479 and 1481. Between the two churches is the 87 meter high tower known as **Lange Jan** (Long John); although it was erected between the 14th and 15th centuries, it is surmounted by an 18th century cusp. Just beyond the abbey is the **Oudhospitaal**, an old military hospital in the Flemish Renaissance style of the 17th century. It has an unusual high sloping roof with painted dormers. Above the central portal of the façade is an imperial eagle with outspread wings. The most impressive view of the city, however, is afforded by an aerial panorama which shows its striking plan, surely the most unusual in all of Holland. The historic center, enclosed within a circular roadway, is surrounded by a double band of star-shaped canals. The plan has been attributed to van Coehoorn, general consultant for the fortifications of the United Provinces in the 17th century and military engineer of the school of Vauban.

The internal courtyard of the Abbey, *the* Oudhospitaal, *the interior of the* Nieuwe Kerk.

These pages and preceding pages:
some sculptures in the Kröller-Müller Museum park.

NIJMEGEN

Nijmegen, nestling on the hills of the left bank of the river Waal, rises on the site of a Batavian "oppidum" which was destroyed in 69 A.D. by the Roman legions who had come to quell a revolt. The Romans then founded a settlement called Noviomagus on the spot which in 105 A.D. Trajan proclaimed a Roman city with the name of Ulpia Noviomagus. Set on a plain overlooking the river is the Valkhof, literally "falcon park", since Charlemagne's son, Louis the Pious, used to raise hunting falcons here. Here too, in 768, Charlemagne had a palace built for himself which soon became one of his favorite residences. Sacked numerous times by the Normans, it was rebuilt by Frederick the Redbeard in 1152. Today, all that is left of the old building, witness to so many historical events, is an octagonal brick baptistery consecrated by Leo III in 799. Despite the addition of a Gothic apse, the name **Carolingian Chapel** has remained to this day.

The Waag *in Nijmegen, two details of the* Grote Kerk, *the* Carolingian chapel.

ARNHEM

According to tradition, a part of the territory of Arnhem rises over the area which Tacitus had called "Arenacum." But whatever the origins of the city may be, it evidently was soon considered an important center, since by the 13th century Otto III, Count of Gelderland, had granted it the status of a city. Its highly favorable position on the right bank of the Neder Rijn (the Lower Rhine) was one of the major factors in stimulating rapid economic development. For almost two hundred years a member of the Hanseatic League, it was taken over by the Dukes of Burgundy when the Gelder dukes died out. It was actually the Emperor Charles V, heir to the Burgundy property, who did most to develop the city's great potential when he decided to set up the high court of justice in Arnhem. Philip II followed suit when he established the administrative courts here. The city continued to prosper until, like all of the other Dutch cities, it was submerged by the fateful events of the 17th and 18th centuries. In 1672 it fell to the French who left it two years later, only to reappear in 1799. Arnhem's name today evokes more recent, but even more tragic memories. In September 1944 an ill-fated landing attempted by a division of British para-

The Grote Kerk, *the* Stadhuis.

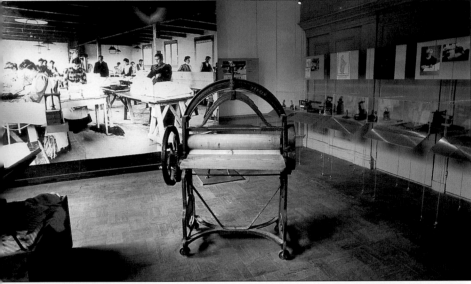

The modern building *behind the Stadhuis, the* Sabelspoort, *two glimpses of the laundry in the* Nederlands Openluchtmuseum.

chutists provoked one of the fiercest battles fought in World War II. The city was destroyed and 7000 of the 10,000 British soldiers engaged in the battle were killed in action. One of the musts on a visit to Arnhem is the **Stadhuis**, popularly known as the Duivelshuis (the House of the Devil). Its incredible sculptural decoration makes it the most unusual sight in the city. Once the home of Maarten van Rossum, the famous general in the service of Charles of Gelderland, it was built between 1539 and 1546 in the Renaissance style. The corner projection leads to the lower floor where there is a portico sustained by three human figures with horse-hoof feet. The façade is decorated with expertly carved human head and body sculptures. The Markt, a huge, modern-day square, contains the city's principal buildings: an old city gate erected in 1357 and the **Grote Kerk**, or the Church of St. Eusebius, a basilica built in the 15th century in the late Gothic style with a lovely tower begun in 1452 by Arend van Gelder. Inside the building is the tomb of Charles of Gelder, a fine Renaissance style work of 1538.

Nederlands Openluchtmuseum

But one of the most fascinating sights in Arnhem – and one that is definitely unique in Holland – is the Openlucht-museum.

The full name of this unusual open-air museum is Rijksmuseum voor Volkskunde Nederlands Openluchtmuseum. It was founded in 1918 by a local historical society with quite an interesting idea in mind: several examples of Netherlandish rural architecture were either transported or reconstructed on 110 acres of park grounds. The visitor may thus follow the evolution of a single style or the birth and development of a tradition. Each building is properly furnished and equipped with all that is required to carry out everyday activities. Thus, by following the route marked out for the sightseer, we can observe all the different kinds of homes from the various provinces: the hut with the straw roof from the Twente region dating from the 1600s (the oldest kind of Saxon rustic dwelling); the hut used by the fishermen of the Volendam area, so tiny it could only be used by a single person at a time, from the north bank of the IJ; the water-mill for the manufacture of paper, an oil plant from Zieuwent; a typical inn, the "De Hanekamp," from the Overijssel region. In the middle of the park there are five different types of windmill, each one built differently and thus used for a different purpose. The ones shown here are of two different kinds; one is a sawmill dating from about 1700 and originally from Dordrecht, while the other was used to drain the polders and was built in 1862 (its drainage capacity is 50-60 m^3 of water per minute). Next to the two mills is a charming group of buildings which once formed the dwelling of a merchant from Koog (on the banks of the river Zaan). The oldest part of the wooden house dates from 1686. Later, other wings were added to the core and the building gradually became what we see today. The interior is in perfect keeping with the bourgeois style that dominated the 19th century. Rather different in style and taste is this rustic farm building from Midlum in Friesland, typical of the region throughout the 17th century. The most interesting parts are the granary, an immense aisled structure rebuilt in 1778, and the kitchen which is com-

pletely furnished with period pieces. During the second half of the 15th century, the invention of printing led to an increase in the consumption of and demand for paper, whereby creating a boom in the paper industry. The technique of using a mill as a power source for the whole range of human activities could hardly be ignored in the development of papermaking. One of the Openluchtmuseum's most fascinating historical relics is a water-mill originally part of a tiny paper-mill in Veluwe in Gelderland, dating from the mid 1800s. From it, we can get an idea of how paper was made a hundred years ago. The power produced by water falling from the mill wheel was used to finely grind linen rags inside a kind of giant mortar equipped with hammers as well as to run the "Dutchman" (a machine with revolving blades in which the resulting linen pulp underwent further mashing). This pulp was then manually drained on wooden frames and a metal strainer until the fibers sedimented and a sheet of paper was obtained. The raw paper was placed between two felt pads and pressed to make the fibers stick together better, and then dried out.

These pages: interior *of a typical house, the* barber's shop, *a* mill *and some* reconstructed houses *at the Nederlands Openluchtmuseum.*

The Bergkerk, *the* Penninckhuis,
the Historisch Museum de Waag.

The Grote Kerk *or Sint Lebuinuskerk,*
the Stadhuis.

The Korenmarktspoort.

KAMPEN

Kampen enjoyed great prosperity throughout the Middle Ages (it belonged to the Hanseatic League) due to its favorable location at the mouth of the IJssel.

Then, with the progressive silting over of the river, and the closing off of the sea inside the city, like numerous other Dutch trading centers, Kampen began its decline.

Three majestic city gates are all that is left of the city's glorious past: the Broderpoort, the Cellenbroederspoort; and the **Korenmarktspoort** with its imposing round flanking towers.

GRONINGEN

Capital of the province of the same name, Groningen is the foremost city of North Holland, especially after the announcement that methane gas deposits were recently discovered in the environs. The city is extremely old: the name Groningen appears for the first time in a bequest made in 1040 by the German Emperor Henry III to the Bishop of Utrecht. Fortified in 1110, its growth was rapid and in 1229 it joined the Hanseatic League. In 1579 it became a member of the Union of Utrecht and fought valiantly against the Spanish who occupied it from 1580 to 1594. At the end of the 17th century it was protected by fortifications, later torn down between 1874 and 1878 to make way for public gardens. Groningen's importance was further enhanced by the founding of a **university** ranking second only to the University of Leyden. Inside the university building is a lovely auditorium with fine stained glass windows by J. Dijkstra and a Senate Hall decorated with the portraits of the professors who taught there. The heart of the city is the marketplace, the Grote Markt, on which we find the neo-classical Stadhuis and the Goudkantoor. The latter has been attributed to Garwer Peters, the same architect responsible for the 17th century fortifications. Today the building is occupied by the Ship Museum which contains fascinating ship models, navigation devices, paintings, anchors, etc. On the northeastern corner of the square originally stood a Romanesque oratory built either in the 11th or 12th century. At the beginning of the 13th century a church dedicated to the protector of the city, St. Martin, was put up in its place. Only the transept is left of the original 13th century church: the choir with its hexagonal plan was built between 1400 and 1425 and subsequent alterations carried out in the 15th century resulted in the nave being enlarged. The church's finest feature, however, is its five story **bell-tower** which is Gothic at the base and Renaissance in the upper stories. The 315 foot tower (just a bit lower than the bell-tower of the Cathedral of Utrecht) commands a magnificent view of the city.

The University *and the* bell-tower *of the Martinikerk.*

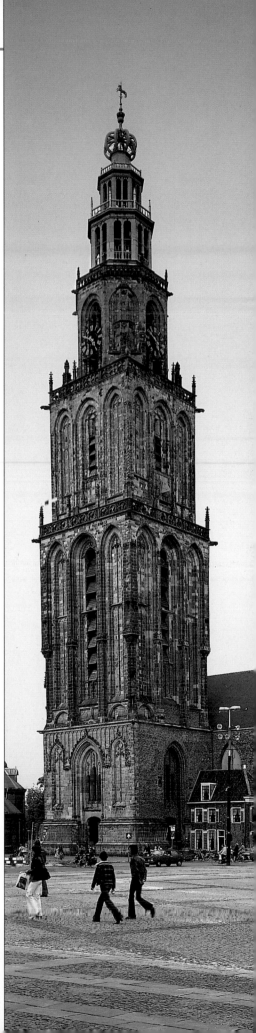

FRIESLAND

Stretching along the banks of the IJsselmeer and the North Sea, the province of Friesland is one of the richest regions in Holland. It was already mentioned by Homer, Pliny the Elder, and Tacitus as a treacherous place always covered by fog – in fact, in 325 B.C. the Greek Pytheas dubbed it the "Coast of Terror." This gives us some idea of how hard life was for the inhabitants of the province. The never-ending struggle waged against the sea and natural forces evidently tempered the character of this hardy people; around 50 B.C. they were even able to revolt against the Roman troops and drive them back beyond the Rhine.

We hardly know anything about the origin of the Frisians, although it is believed that they originally came from the Scandinavian peninsula (perhaps Sweden) or that they were of Celtic origin. Nevertheless, it is a fact that the language they speak, while practically incomprehensible to most of the Dutch, is quite similar to the English spoken by the inhabitants of Yorkshire – it is even said that the Yorkshire fishermen can understand their Frisian counterparts. Rigorously autonomous throughout Dutch history (and right through the war against Spain in which the rest of the country was passionately involved), the Frisians also dif-

fer from the rest of the population with regards to their eth-
nic characteristics; their light complexions, blond hair, blue
eyes, and tall stature make them much more Scandinavian
looking than the rest of the population. They also have their
own national anthem and their own flag, which is blue and
white with red leaves.
The Frisians earn their living primarily from cattle breeding,
raising the famous **Frisian cows**. These cows, which an old
country tradition calls the "great mothers", are the world's
greatest milk producers. The butter made from this milk,
along with English butter, is supposedly the best in the
world – or so an old Dutch saying goes.

But Friesland is not only renowned for its agricultural produce. The region is in fact a paradise for boat lovers. The whole countryside is dotted with hundreds of little lakes ventilated by sea breezes which, especially on weekends, come alive with all kinds of sailboats, canoes and rowboats.

Besides sailing, the Dutch love skating, which is their national winter sport.

The skating champions all compete in an unusual (and exhausting) race, the Elfstedentocht (11-city race), which entails skating over 200 kilometers.

The sea and lakes of Friesland *are ideal for sailing entusiasts.*

CONTENTS